HEADLINES FROM HISTORY ™

America's First Traitor
Benedict Arnold Betrays the Colonies

Allison Stark Draper

The Rosen Publishing Group's
PowerKids Press™
New York

For my father

Published in 2001 by The Rosen Publishing Group, Inc.
29 East 21st Street, New York, NY 10010

First Edition

Book Design: Michael de Guzman

Photo Credits: pp. 4, 8, 11, 21 © North Wind Picture Archives; p. 7 CORBIS/Bettmann; pp. 12, 17 by MaryJane Wojciechowski; p. 15 by Tim Hall; p. 18 © Bettmann/CORBIS.

Draper, Allison Stark.
    America's first traitor : Benedict Arnold betrays the colonies / Allison Stark Draper.
       p. cm.— (Headlines from history)
    Includes index.
    Summary: This book describes the military successes of Benedict Arnold in the Colonial Army, his disappointments in personal promotions, and eventually his betrayal of the colonies.
    ISBN 0-8239-5673-3
    1. Arnold, Benedict, 1741–1801—Juvenile literature. 2. American loyalists—Biography—Juvenile literature. 3. Generals—United States—Biography—Juvenile literature. 4. United States—Continental Army—Biography—Juvenile literature. 5. United States—History—Revolution, 1775–1783—Juvenile literature. [1.Arnold, Benedict, 1741–1801. 2. American loyalists. 3. Generals. 4. United States—History—Revolution, 1775–1783—Biography.] I. Title. II. Series.

E278.A7 D73 2000
973.3'82'092—dc21
[B]   00-026175

Manufactured in the United States of America

C O N T E N T S

Benedict Arnold Joins Fight Against British Rule

Benedict Arnold was born on January 14, 1741. His family lived in Connecticut. Connecticut was a British **colony**. This means that the people living there had to follow British laws even though they were in a new land.

4

Arnold was trained to be an **apothecary**. An apothecary prepared and sold medicine. In 1763, Arnold opened his own store. During that time, the British **colonists** began speaking out against British rule. The colonists now thought of themselves as **independent.** They did not want to follow British laws any longer. They also did not want to pay money to the British government. The war for American independence, called the Revolutionary War, started. Arnold helped America fight the British. He became a captain in the **militia**.

Benedict Arnold joined the fight for American independence from England.

5

Fort Ticonderoga Falls

The Revolutionary War began in April 1775. Benedict Arnold decided to attack a British **fort** called Fort Ticonderoga. At the same time, a **patriot** named Ethan Allen also decided to attack the fort. Allen led a group of men called the Green Mountain Boys. Arnold was angry. He wanted to capture the fort on his own. Arnold could not make Allen give up his plan to attack the fort. Arnold finally agreed to fight alongside Allen's men. On May 10, 1775, the Americans **captured** the British fort. The American army gave Ethan Allen credit for the attack. Arnold felt that he was not being treated fairly.

American patriot Ethan Allen was born in Connecticut in 1738.

6

Benedict Arnold Leads March on Canada

George Washington was a general in the American army. In the fall of 1775, he took command of the American troops. General Washington, who later became the first

8

president of the United States, trusted Benedict Arnold. Washington asked Arnold to lead an attack against the British in Quebec, Canada. Arnold's 1,100 soldiers would reach Canada by going through Maine. Another army of American soldiers would attack Canada from New York. The two groups of soldiers would meet in Quebec.

On September 21, 1775, Arnold's men boarded 200 riverboats. It rained a lot on their trip. The men were cold and hungry. They got so hungry that they had to boil their leather shoes to make soup. Many men died. Others left without permission. In November 1775, Arnold arrived in Quebec with 650 men.

This picture shows Benedict Arnold and his men traveling through Maine to reach Canada.

9

American Forces Lose in Quebec

When Arnold and his men got to Canada it was raining hard. Arnold wrote to General George Washington. He said that his soldiers were not able to move because of the bad weather. Washington never got the letter. An Indian spy gave it to the British. The British sent more men to Quebec to make the British army even stronger. Arnold had to wait for more American soldiers. Three hundred American troops finally arrived. On December 31, 1775, Arnold's troops attacked Quebec.

This map is a copy of one made in 1760. Benedict Arnold used this map to help him get from Maine to Canada.

10

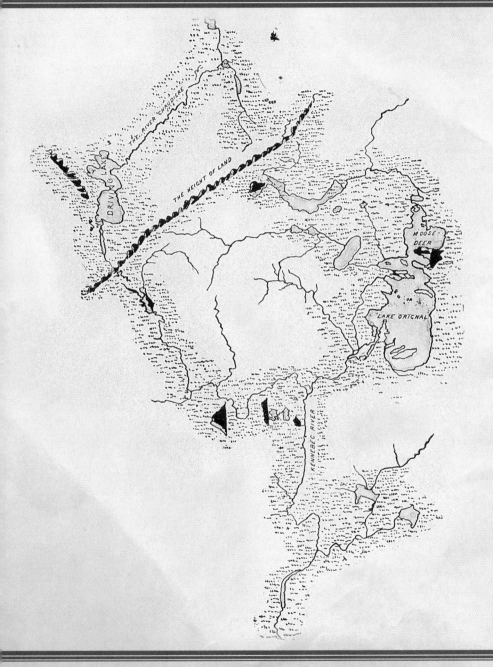

One hundred Americans were killed in the attack. The British also captured 426 men. Arnold was wounded in the leg, but he kept fighting the British. The Americans finally had to give up. The **expedition** had been a failure. Still, General Washington told Arnold that he had been a strong leader.

11

Arnold Finds Out How British Plan to Win War

In June of 1776, Benedict Arnold and his American troops left Canada. The Americans had started out with 200 riverboats, but now had only one left. Arnold

12

and his men had been the first to attack the British in Canada. They were the last to leave Canada nearly a year later.

The British had a plan that they thought would win the war. They were going to trap the Americans between the British troops in the north and the British troops in the south. The British troops in the north would cross Lake Champlain by ship. The Americans didn't have a chance to win against so many British troops. Arnold told the Americans they had to make the British wait through the winter. With that extra time, the American army could get strong enough to beat the British.

Benedict Arnold and his troops were the last Americans to leave Canada.

13

Benedict Arnold Tricks the British

The Americans had a lot fewer ships than the British. Benedict Arnold knew that the head of the British navy was a **cautious** man. If he thought the Americans had a lot of ships, the British would build more. The British would have to spend the winter in Canada building these ships. This would give the Americans time to gather more soldiers and supplies.

Arnold sailed his few ships to the Richelieu River. This was where the British were preparing for battle. The ships fired their cannons. This tricked the British into thinking that the Americans had many ships. The British decided to spend the winter building more ships.

On October 11, 1776, the British navy sailed out to

14

meet the Americans. During the battle, hundreds of Americans were killed. That night Arnold and his men got away from the British. They had lost the battle, but Arnold's plan was still a success. While the British spent the winter building ships, the Americans had time to build up their army.

The Americans fired the cannons from the few ships they had. This tricked the British into thinking that the American navy was bigger than it was.

15

Arnold Leaves the Army

In April of 1777, the British attacked the town of Danbury, Connecticut. Arnold got together a group of people from Connecticut to fight the British. These men were not used to fighting. Some got scared and ran away. Arnold convinced many of the Americans to keep fighting. They won the battle against the British. Arnold's horse fell on top of him during the battle. A British soldier yelled at Arnold to give up. Even though Arnold was trapped under his horse, he pulled out his gun and killed the British soldier. Arnold thought he had done a good job leading his troops. He wanted the American army to give him a **promotion**. When Arnold did not get a promotion, he was upset. He left the American army in July of 1777.

16

Benedict Arnold was a brave soldier. Even though he was trapped under his horse, he kept fighting.

Americans Beat British in Saratoga

After Arnold left the army, he missed being part of the fight for independence. He joined the army again and won a battle against the British at Fort Schuyler in New York. Arnold thought the Americans should attack the British in Saratoga, New York. The general in charge of the American army at Saratoga was Horatio Gates. General Gates did not want

18

Arnold to attack the British. In the fall of 1777, Arnold went into battle anyway. Arnold's troops ended up winning the battle against the British at Saratoga.

Louis XVI, the king of France, heard the news that the Americans had won the Battle of Saratoga. France had lost a war to the British in 1763. This war was called the French and Indian War. King Louis XVI was still angry at the British government. After the Battle of Saratoga, the French thought the Americans might win the Revolutionary War. King Louis XVI decided to send French soldiers to help the Americans.

King Louis XVI of France decided to help the Americans once he thought they might win the war against the British.

19

Benedict Arnold Court-Martialed

After the Battle of Saratoga, General George Washington put Arnold in charge of the city of Philadelphia. While Arnold was in Philadelphia, he ran out of money. He took wagons from the government. He used them for his own business. This was not legal. The army **court-martialed** him. He was found guilty of two crimes but was not put in jail. Even after the court-martial, Washington thought Arnold was a good soldier.

Arnold, though, was angry and bitter. He had spent his own money fighting the war. The army paid him back, but Arnold thought he was owed more money. The British knew Arnold

After the war, George Washington became the first president of the United States.

was angry with the Americans. The British thought Arnold might help them beat the Americans if they paid him money. Arnold agreed to take money to help the British win the war.

George Washington offered Arnold another job in the American army. Arnold refused. He had a plan to help the British. He said he wanted to be in charge of West Point, New York.

21

Arnold Betrays America

In 1780, Arnold was put in charge of the fort at West Point. He had a plan to help the British win the war. The British would attack West Point. Arnold would pretend to fight the British, but then give up. A British officer on his way to meet Arnold was caught by the Americans. He was carrying papers signed by Arnold. This proved that Arnold was working for England. The British officer was hanged for being a **spy.** Arnold ran away to England. The British paid Arnold even though his plan did not work out. They did not trust him, though. He could not find work. He died alone in London in 1801.

Arnold was a brave soldier, but he **betrayed** his country. He will always be remembered as America's first **traitor.**

GLOSSARY

apothecary (uh-POTH-eh-karee) A person who makes and sells medicine.

betrayed (bee-TRAYD) Turned against.

captured (KAP-churd) To have taken over land or control of people.

cautious (KAW-shush) Very careful.

colonists (KAH-luh-nists) People who live in a colony.

colony (KAH-luh-nee) An area in a new country where a large group of people move who are still ruled by the leaders and laws of their old country.

court-martialed (KORT-mar-shuld) A trial for a member of the army, navy, or air force.

expedition (EK-spuh-DIH-shun) A trip for a special purpose.

fort (FORT) A strong building or place that can be defended against an enemy.

independent (in-dih-PEN-dent) To be free from the control, support, or help of other people.

militia (muh-LIH-shuh) A group of people who are trained and ready to fight, but who are not the army.

patriot (PAY-tree-ot) A person who loves and defends his or her country.

promotion (proh-MOH-shun) A raise in rank or importance.

spy (SPY) Someone who watches something secretly.

traitor (TRAY-tor) Someone who turns against his or her own country.

23

INDEX

WEB SITES

To find out more about Benedict Arnold, check out these Web sites:

http://www.libertynet.org/iha/valleyforge/served/arnold.html
http://www.heroswelcome.com/Arnold.htm